MY GUIDE TO
US CITIZENSHIP

YOUR GUIDE TO
BECOMING A
US CITIZEN

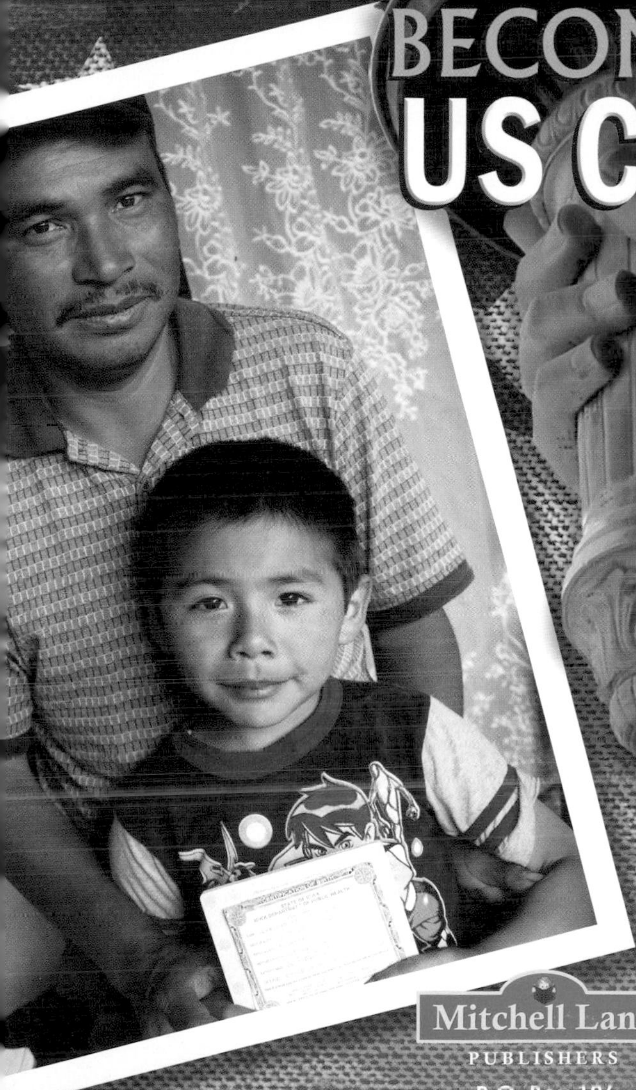

Tammy
Gagne

Mitchell Lane
PUBLISHERS
P.O. Box 196
Hockessin, DE 19707
www.mitchelllane.com

Mitchell Lane
PUBLISHERS

MY GUIDE TO US CITIZENSHIP

Immigration in the US
US Immigration Services
US Laws of Citizenship
Your Guide to Becoming a US Citizen

Copyright © 2014 by Mitchell Lane Publishers

Printing   1   2   3   4   5   6   7   8   9

PUBLISHER'S NOTE: The facts on which this book is based have been thoroughly researched. Documentation of such research can be found on page 44. While every possible effort has been made to ensure accuracy, the publisher will not assume liability for damages caused by inaccuracies in the data, and makes no warranty on the accuracy of the information contained herein.

The Internet sites referenced herein were active as of the publication date. Due to the fleeting nature of some web sites, we cannot guarantee that they will all be active when you are reading this book.

Library of Congress
Cataloging-in-Publication Data

Gagne, Tammy.
 Your guide to becoming a US citizen / by Tammy Gagne.
   pages cm. — (My guide to US citizenship)
 Includes bibliographical references and index.
 ISBN 978-1-61228-449-1 (library bound)
 1. Naturalization—United States—Juvenile literature. 2. Citizenship—United States—Juvenile literature. I. Title. II. Title: Your guide to becoming a United States citizen.
 KF4710.Z9G34 2013
 323.6'230973—dc23
                                        2013023025
e-Book ISBN: 9781612285092

                                        PLB

CONTENTS

Words in **bold** appear in the Glossary.

The decision to apply for United States citizenship is a big one. The naturalization process takes both time and effort. Applicants must learn the English language. They also must learn about American history and government. For those who want it most, though, becoming a citizen is a proud achievement.

The Decision to Become a US Citizen

Regina stood in the front row of the large courtroom with her right hand raised in the air. She could not keep her eyes off the striking red, white, and blue flag that hung before her and the other soon-to-be new United States citizens. This important symbol would now belong as much to her as to every other American. The room fell silent as everyone prepared to take their Oath of Allegiance. This final step would make the **naturalization** process official. Regina had dreamed of this day for many years, from the time she had first arrived in this country from her native town of Lecheria in Sonora, Mexico. Back then she couldn't even speak English. She felt a tear slip down her cheek. She knew without a doubt that she would remember this day for as long as she lived.

5

Deciding to become a US citizen is a big decision. Many people who come to the United States from other countries never take this giant step. More than fifteen million US naturalized citizens lived in the United States as of 2011, and another 9.7 million **immigrants** were **eligible** to apply for citizenship.[1] Still, many of these people will choose to live in the United States for the rest of their lives without ever becoming US citizens. They may worry that applying for citizenship here means turning their backs on their native country or on the family members still living there. Others worry that naturalization is expensive or that the test is too difficult. Some may see no reason to apply for citizenship.

Whether you have arrived in the United States recently or you have lived here for many years, there are numerous advantages to becoming a US citizen. Immigrants who become citizens do not have to worry about being deported, the technical term for being removed from the country. Green cards, the identification documents that allow immigrants to legally and permanently live in the United States, are only good for ten years. Before those ten years are up, immigrant residents must apply for a renewal.

Naturalized citizens can also travel out of the United States freely, returning whenever they choose. Many people from countries all over the world dream of living in the United States, but being away from loved ones for long periods of time can be difficult for anyone. Non-citizens who travel home to visit family and friends may find their permanent resident status revoked if they wish to come back to the United States after an extended absence.

Something else to consider when deciding to become a US citizen is the ever-changing world of politics. Various governors, members of Congress, and even presidents disagree about immigration and citizenship laws. By becoming a citizen now, you won't have to worry about any changes

that are made to the immigration or naturalization process in the future.

Citizenship entitles a naturalized American to nearly all the same benefits that natural-born citizens possess. One thing a naturalized citizen cannot do is serve as president. Article 2, Section 1, Clause 5 of the US Constitution states, "No Person except a natural born Citizen, or a Citizen of the United States, at the time of the Adoption of this Constitution, shall be eligible to the Office of President; neither shall any Person be eligible to that Office who shall not have attained to the Age of thirty five Years, and been fourteen Years a Resident within the United States."[2]

Naturalized citizens can, however, run for other types of public office. Immigrants who become citizens also win the right to vote in both local and national elections. Many people come to the United States from countries that offer their citizens no voice in their own government at all. Some of these people travel great distances and endure great hardship just to make it to the United States. Here, they have the opportunity to be heard. Not everyone who immigrates to the United States wants to be involved in the political process, but the fact that they have the right to do so is something very special to many new American citizens.

The benefits of becoming a US citizen are undeniable, but there are also a few disadvantages for some immigrants. Many countries, like the United States, allow their people to hold citizenship in more than one country at the same time.

> You must be eighteen years of age to apply for US citizenship. If you were born in the United States—even if your parents were not citizens at the time, however, you do not need to be naturalized. You already have what is called birthright citizenship.

Others, however, do not. If you come from a country that doesn't allow dual citizenship, you will need to choose between remaining a citizen of your native country and being naturalized.

Becoming a US citizen can also prevent you from serving your native country in the event of war. Part of the naturalization process is swearing an oath to the United States. The oath begins, "I hereby declare, on oath, that I absolutely and entirely renounce and abjure all allegiance and fidelity to any foreign prince, potentate, state or sovereignty, of whom or which I have heretofore been a subject or citizen; that I will support and defend the Constitution and laws of the United States of America against all enemies, foreign and domestic . . . "[3] Because of this oath, a naturalized US citizen cannot fight for his or her native country in a war against the United States or any other country it supports.

In certain situations, applying for citizenship in the United States can also increase your chance of being removed from the country. Some immigrants want to enter the United States so badly that they lie when filling out their green card applications. Other times mistakes are made by the US Citizenship and Immigration Service (USCIS). When the USCIS approves a green card application for a person who isn't truly eligible to become a legal immigrant, chances are good that the error will be caught if that person applies for citizenship.

Even if no mistakes were made when you received your green card, committing a crime can keep you from becoming a US citizen. All people who live in the United States are expected to follow its laws. Violating the law or the conditions of your green card can not only cause your application for citizenship to be denied, but it will also increase your chance of being deported.

If you are a legal immigrant, you can enlist in the United States military before you become a citizen. Immigrants who enlist may be able to complete the naturalization process more quickly than normal—sometimes in just a few weeks. Homeland Security Secretary Janet Napolitano shares, "Since 2001, US Citizenship and Immigration Services has naturalized over eighty thousand members of the armed forces, bringing immigration services to our troops wherever they serve. And since 2009, we have offered non-citizen enlistees the opportunity to naturalize before completing basic training so they can graduate as American citizens."[4]

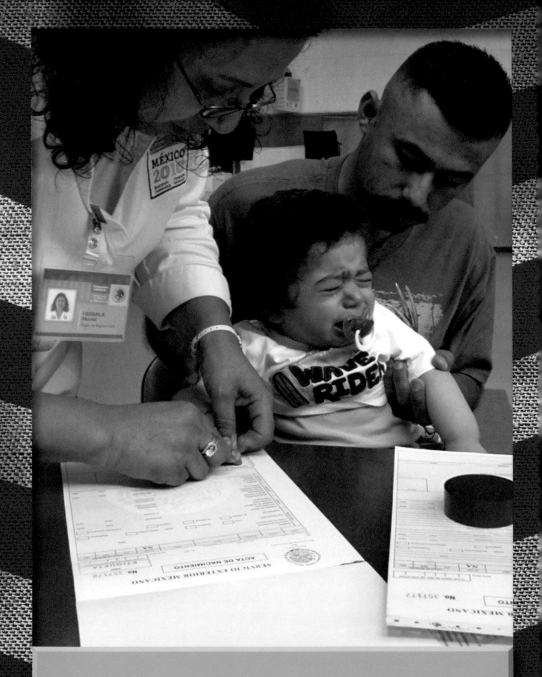

Saul Arias is already an American citizen, since he was born in Santa Barbara, California. But his father Victor is from Nayarit, Mexico, and wants his son to have dual citizenship—citizenship in both Mexico and the United States. Here, Saul's fingerprints are taken at the Mexican consulate in Santa Barbara.

Are You Eligible for Citizenship?

Before you can apply for US citizenship, you must find out if you are in fact eligible for naturalization. The first requirement to be naturalized is a green card. If you do not have a green card, you must get one before you can apply for citizenship.

It is important to point out that getting a green card is often a very difficult task. Some immigrants struggle to get this important document for years. In 2011, a young woman named Atossa Araxia Abrahamian was among those denied a green card. She had entered the *green card lottery* the previous year. Also called the diversity lottery, this process grants fifty-five thousand green cards each year to people from countries with low rates of immigration to the United States. "They call it a lottery

11

The diversity lottery draws many people who wouldn't otherwise be eligible for a green card. The lottery was created to encourage immigrants to come to the United States from countries with low rates of immigration. Before people could apply for this lottery online, crowds waited in long lines to enter their names. Here, a crowd waits outside the Federal Office building in New York, 1996.

for good reason," Abrahamian explains; "the odds of winning are **minute**."[1]

Interestingly, she did win, but still she was not granted permanent resident status. On the application she had claimed her country of origin to be Switzerland (where she grew up) instead of Canada (where she was born). This error cost Abrahamian her green card.

"I used to think of immigration as a problem for the migrant poor, not something that affected college-educated global citizens," she shares. "I now know that getting a work permit is a complicated and often heartbreaking process, no matter who you are. Thanks to months of pitching articles to whoever would let me write them—not to mention a good lawyer—I finally obtained an O visa this year. I don't have to get married, to a man or a job, to have a career in the United States. But I was able to stay only because I had the

In 2012, President Barack Obama announced a new program to help young immigrants who came to the United States as children. In this program, immigrants who met certain criteria were allowed to stay in the country for an additional two years, and could receive work permits. Hundreds of thousands of people, like these immigrants in Los Angeles, responded to the program.

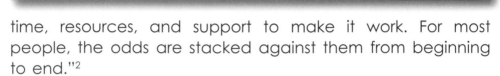

If you are under eighteen, you may become a United States citizen under certain circumstances. First, you must be a legal permanent resident of the United States. Second, at least one of your parents must become a naturalized citizen while you are still underage. And finally, he or she must also have legal and physical custody of you.

time, resources, and support to make it work. For most people, the odds are stacked against them from beginning to end."[2]

Once you have a green card, you must continue to be a resident of the United States for at least five years before filing for naturalization. During this time, you cannot leave the country for more than six months out of each year. Exceptions to the five-year rule can be made in certain cases. For instance, an immigrant may become eligible for citizenship three years after he or she marries a US citizen. In this case, the spouse must have been a citizen for at least three years prior to filing the application.

Depending on what you do for a living, you may also get special permission to leave the United States for more than six months if it's required for your job. You must live in the country for at least one full year before leaving, though. You also need to return no later than two and a half years after leaving.

You may move from one state or USCIS district to another during the time you live in the United States. Before applying for citizenship, though, you must have lived in the same state or district for at least three months. Also, as mentioned previously, you must be at least eighteen years of age before filing your citizenship application.

The law states that all immigrants who apply for citizenship must be able to speak, read, and write English. A USCIS employee will judge these skills during an interview. Immigrants fifty years old or older who have lived in the United States for

In Tuscon, Arizona, the public schools' Pan Asian Studies Department developed a program in which students of Vietnamese descent help elder Vietnamese immigrants study for their citizenship exams. Here, high school senior Mymy Bui (*middle*) helps Kim Phuong (*left*) pronounce a sentence in English.

at least twenty years can request a 50/20 **waiver**. This allows a person's interview to be given in his or her native language. A 55/15 waiver does the same thing for people fifty-five and older who have lived in the United States for at least fifteen years.

Waivers can also be given in the case of a disability that makes learning English especially difficult. It is important to

Not everyone who applies to become a US citizen is approved. Anna Yaksich arrived in the United States from Yugoslavia in 1907, when she was just five years old. Throughout her life, she tried to become a citizen, but was turned down. Here, she holds her denial letter, which states that the government could not verify her entry into the United States.

understand that these are exceptions, though. In the case of a disability, a doctor must fill out an N-648 form to request a waiver. In it, he or she must explain how the particular disability affects the person's ability to learn English.

In addition to English, applicants must also learn basic information about the history of the United States and its government before becoming a US citizen. You will need to pass an oral exam on these subjects in order to have your naturalization application approved. This portion of the citizenship test is often referred to as the civics portion.

Waivers relating to age and disabilities also exist for taking this test in your native language. In addition to the 50/20 and 55/15 waivers, the history and government exam offers a 65/20 waiver. This allows people sixty-five and older to study a smaller number of questions and take the test in their native language.

In order to be eligible for citizenship, you must demonstrate that you possess good moral character. This means that you contribute to the community in a positive way, by following the law or paying your taxes, for example. Any crimes that you have committed will be considered as part of determining whether you fulfill this requirement. One of the most important ways you can demonstrate good moral character is by telling the truth on your application and in your interview. If you lie, the USCIS will likely deny your application.

Finally, all immigrants applying for citizenship must be willing to pledge their loyalty to the United States. As part of the naturalization process, you will be required to swear the Oath of Allegiance to the United States. You can also show your loyalty and respect in the way you speak about the country and the US Constitution.

The USCIS actually allows eligible immigrants to apply for citizenship as early as ninety days before their required residency period is completed. You won't be able to become a citizen any earlier, but filing early will allow the USCIS to begin processing your paperwork as soon as possible.

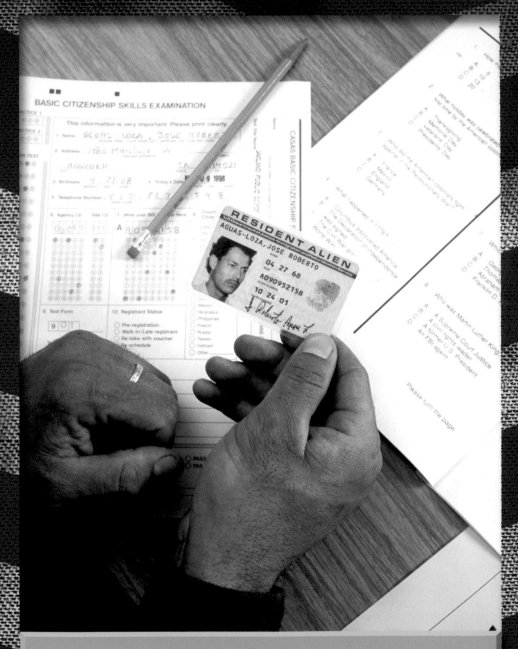

A green card is the first step to becoming a United States citizen. This document gives an immigrant permission to live and work in the United States on a permanent basis. Once an immigrant has been a permanent resident for five continuous years, he or she may then apply to become a naturalized citizen.

The Application Process

If you want to become a US citizen—and you are eligible—the next step is filling out your application. The form you will need is called the N-400. You can find it at the US Citizenship and Immigration Services website. You can also get a hard copy of this form by calling USCIS at (800) 870-3676.

In addition to filling out the form, you will also need to copy various documents to submit along with it. One document everyone must submit is a copy of his or her green card. Be sure to make a copy of both the front and back of this document on two separate sheets of full-sized paper.

The other documents and the number of copies you must send will be unique to your situation. Be prepared to bring the original documents with you to your interview, though. It is also very important to send English translations of any documents written in a foreign language. Translations should be done by a person **fluent** in both languages, and this person must also state in writing that their translation is correct. Even a small error could make all the difference in the approval of your application.

In addition to copies of your official documents, you also need to include two identical color photographs of yourself with your application. You might be tempted to use a photo you already have or to have a friend snap a quick picture, but neither option is a smart choice. Instead, find a business that takes passport photos. Doing so will ensure that your photos meet the USCIS's requirements. Photos need to be taken within thirty days of the date that you mail your application. You will also need to write your name and green card number on the back of each photo in pencil. Do this very gently to avoid damaging the photographs.

The purpose of the N-400 is to gather as much information as possible about you. It begins by asking for your name. It then covers all the details that prove you are indeed eligible to become a US citizen. You will be asked questions about your residence and employment, any criminal records, and any time you have spent outside the United States since your

Applicants must include legal proof of any name change with their applications for citizenship. A person who has gotten married or divorced since receiving his or her green card must make a copy of the marriage certificate or divorce decree. A copy of the document should be included with the application, and the original document should be taken to the citizenship interview.

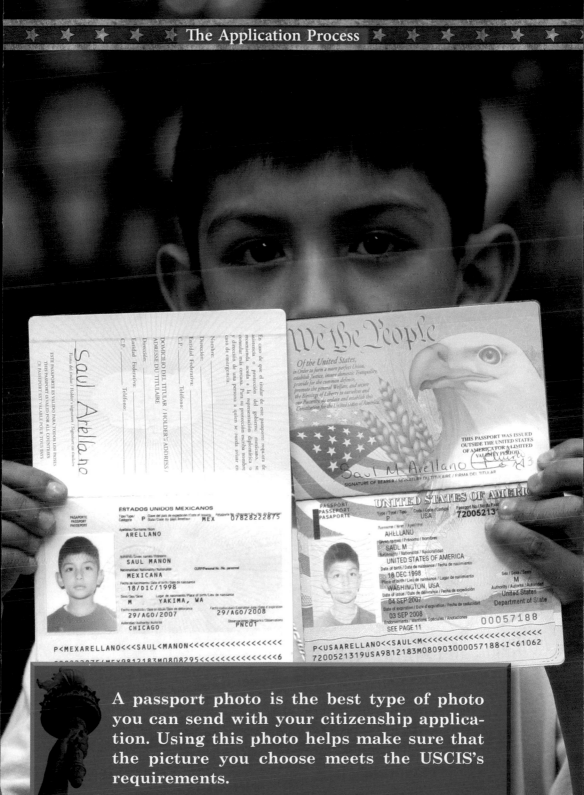

A passport photo is the best type of photo you can send with your citizenship application. Using this photo helps make sure that the picture you choose meets the USCIS's requirements.

residency began. It also includes questions about your military history, marriages, and children.

Filling out the N-400 can be difficult for someone who is new to the English language. Even for people who are fluent in English, this form can be overwhelming. The best thing you can do is to relax and take it slowly. Rushing or letting your nerves take over will only increase your chances of making a mistake. If you aren't sure how to answer a question, get help. If you can afford it, it may be worth the extra expense of hiring an immigration lawyer to help you with your paperwork. If money is a concern, you may be able to find a legal organization in your area that offers its services for free to people in your situation.

The last thing you must include with your application is payment for your application fee. This may be paid in the form of a cashier's check or a money order, but a personal check is better because it is the easiest to trace. Make it payable to US Department of Homeland Security, and be sure to spell out all the words completely. You will need to send a total of $680—including $595 for your citizenship application fee and $85 for the cost of fingerprinting. You will be contacted at a later date with instructions for the time and place to have your fingerprints taken.

Just as there are exceptions to other parts of the naturalization process, the application fee also has its exceptions. For example, members of the US military do not need to pay either fee. People seventy-five and older do not have to pay the $85 fingerprinting fee, as they do not have to be fingerprinted. People living overseas for their jobs also don't have to include the $85 fingerprinting fee. They can have this step performed at their US consulate or military base, and include the fingerprint cards with the application instead.

Becoming a citizen is expensive. In 2007 the application fee increased by 69 percent.[1] This extreme increase caused a spike in applications for citizenship from people trying to get their applications in before the new rate went into effect. Since the price increase, however, the number of applications has dropped severely. Many people blame the increased fee for the decrease in the number of people applying for

An experienced immigration attorney who is familiar with the naturalization forms and application requirements can help make the naturalization process a smooth one. Here, attorney Monica Salazar (*left*) helps Seung and Hyun Lee with their citizenship applications in Nampa, Idaho.

citizenship. And since fees can change at any time, make sure you verify the fees on the USCIS website before you apply.

If you cannot afford the application fee, the USCIS may agree to waive the fee. In order to qualify for this benefit, your income must fall below 150 percent of the federal **poverty level**. This number can change from year to year, so check the USCIS website for the exact amount. You can also find this information at the US Department of Health and Human Services website. If you are able to prove that you have a financial hardship situation, such as high medical bills, this might also qualify you for a fee waiver.

If you will be taking advantage of any exceptions, you must include copies of additional documents. For example, an immigrant who has been married to a US citizen for three or more years must provide proof of the spouse's citizenship. A copy of the marriage certificate will also be needed.

It is wise to include a cover letter with your application. In it, you should clearly state your situation, including any exceptions. You should also note these exceptions on your application, so there is no chance that they can be missed. For example, you should write "Fee Waiver Requested" on

Many people worry that they won't be given the fee waiver they request. To save time some of them include a check, asking that it only be cashed if the waiver is denied. Unfortunately, including a check shows USCIS that you can actually afford to pay the fee. Since the fee waiver is intended for people who cannot afford the fee, including the extra check is the best way to make sure your waiver request is indeed denied.

In New York City, a nonprofit organization called Citizenship Now! helps thousands of immigrants with the citizenship process. Its Express Center in the Washington Heights neighborhood offers free legal assistance to immigrants who want to become US citizens. Here, Angel and Evie Gomez meet with attorney Andres Lemons. Although the couple is about to have a baby in the US, neither parent is a citizen—yet. Angel is from the Dominican Republic, and Evie is from Canada. Both plan to apply for citizenship.

both the top of the N-400 form and on the outside of your mailing envelope. It is better to include too much information than too little. And be sure to make photocopies of your entire application for your own records before mailing it off.

Be sure to check your mail regularly after filing your citizenship application. If you sent your paperwork by certified mail with return receipt, you will receive a green postcard notifying you that your application was delivered. You should also receive a letter from the USCIS within a couple of weeks confirming that they have received your paperwork.

Waiting—and Waiting Some More

Once your citizenship application has been received and reviewed, the next big step is your interview. Like so many things in life, worrying about this meeting is often far more stressful than the actual event. Oftentimes the hardest part is waiting to hear from the USCIS. The longer you must wait, the more you may worry. Luckily, there are a few things you can do to ease your nerves during this time.

The most important thing you can do to ensure that everything will go smoothly is to fill out your application properly. After that, your biggest goal should be making sure that the application makes it to the USCIS. Mail your application by certified mail with a return receipt. Your local post office will have the necessary forms, including a green postcard that you must address to yourself. When the USCIS receives the envelope, this postcard will be mailed back to you to confirm receipt of the documents. You should receive it in about fourteen days from the time you mailed your

After you send your documents by certified mail, the post office will issue you a receipt like this one. This is your proof that your application was sent.

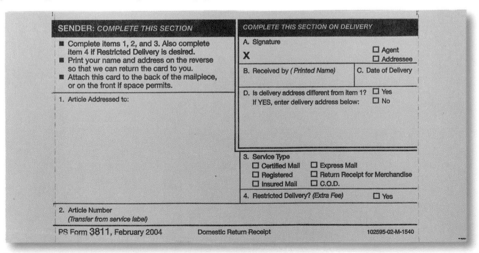

A return receipt will be mailed back to you when the USCIS has received your application.

application. You will pay a little extra for certified mail, but it will be worth it to have proof that your application has been received.

Another form of proof that the agency has received your application is the cancelled check for the application fee. If you have this item, you know that everything is moving in the right direction. If you don't receive cancelled checks from your bank, you can look at your bank statement for proof that the check has indeed been cashed.

You should also receive written confirmation that the USCIS has received your application within two weeks or so. This letter will include your file's receipt number. Keep this number handy, as it should be included on any future paperwork.

The wait time between applying for citizenship and being interviewed varies from area to area. It can even be different between cities in the same state. The goal of the USCIS is to process all applications within five months, but this is not a guarantee. The processing time of each office depends on how many applications they receive and how many people they have to work on them. It can take even longer to receive your interview date if any problems arise.

One of the most common reasons that the interview process is delayed is missing information on the citizenship application. If you missed a question or forgot to include a copy of a necessary document, you will be notified. Respond by sending the requested information immediately. Like the

When you mail your N-400 form, you can submit form G-1145 along with it to receive updates to your case status by text or email. You can also use your receipt number to check your case status online at the USCIS website.

original application, any additional information you send should be sent by certified mail.

Don't panic if you are notified of missing material that you are certain you included with your original application. Unfortunately, the government sometimes misplaces paperwork. Investigative reporters have found that the number of lost immigration files may be as high as eighty thousand in a single year.[1] When this happens, the applicants have to resubmit the information. This is one reason why it's a good idea to keep a copy of your application for your own records. As long as you have proof of your payment, though, you won't have to pay the application fee more than once.

A few weeks after the USCIS receives your application, you will be given a date and time for your **biometrics** appointment. Although it sounds complicated, this is simply the official term for fingerprinting. If at all possible, you should take the first biometrics appointment you are given. Rescheduling this step will only lengthen the wait time for your interview—and for citizenship.

The USCIS allows people to submit applications even before they have learned to speak, read, and write English. They must, however, be able to do so by the time of their interviews. While five months may seem like enough time to learn what you need to know, it may be smarter to wait until you are confident that you can conduct your interview and take your tests in English. You will have two chances to complete your interview and exams successfully. If you cannot complete your interview in English on your second try, you will have to reapply for citizenship. This includes paying the application fee a second time as well.

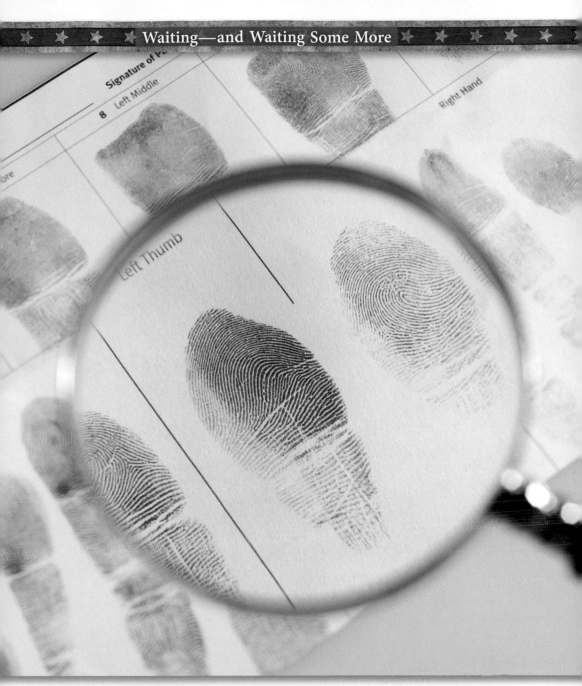

Once the Federal Bureau of Investigations (FBI) has reviewed your fingerprints, this agency will report their findings to the USCIS. The FBI's job in this case is to make sure that your prints are not linked to any crimes. Once this step has been completed and the USCIS has received the results, the USCIS will give you a date for your interview.

The last step to becoming a US citizen is taking part in a naturalization ceremony and taking the Oath of Allegiance. Here Dario Caravati holds the certificate he received at his naturalization ceremony. Dario was born in Italy, but he became an American citizen on June 4, 2010.

Passing the Tests

Chapter 5

Your English skills will be tested during your interview. For the spoken part of your test, you must understand what the interviewer says to you. You also must be able to respond clearly to the interviewer in English. Before you begin, the interviewer will place you under oath to tell the truth. After that, he or she will ask you to have a seat. By following these instructions, you are demonstrating to the interviewer that you understand his or her words.

During the meeting, the interviewer will review your application with you as another way of assessing your English skills. It is very important that the answers you provide during the interview match the information you wrote on your application. Certainly, the answers do not have to match word for

33

word, but nothing you say should conflict with your application. If you made a copy of your application before sending it in, you could prepare by reviewing it.

As hard as it may seem, try to relax during your interview. The interviewer is a person just like you are. Don't worry if you come across an English word that you don't understand. Even people who speak English as their first language do not know every single word in the English language. It is perfectly fine to ask the interviewer to use a different word instead of the one you do not understand.

Speak slowly, and use complete sentences whenever possible. Many times this can be done by repeating part of the question in your answer. If the interviewer says, "How long have you lived in the United States?" you may be tempted to offer a simple response such as, "ten years." You will be able to show off your English skills better by saying, "I have lived in the United States for ten years now."

The reading portion of your interview will be short. The interviewer will give you a piece of writing to read out loud.

If your citizenship application is denied, you will receive a written explanation from the USCIS. At this point you may choose to reapply if your circumstances regarding the denial have changed. You also have the right to appeal the decision by filling out an N-336 form. If you were denied because you failed your exam twice, the best choice may be to study more and apply again when you are confident that you can perform better on the tests. If you don't understand why you were denied citizenship—or if you feel that you were treated unfairly—it may be time to contact an immigration lawyer for help.

Some of the words used in this part of the test may relate to US government and history. Chances are good that you have been studying them for your test in those subjects. If you can read the first sentence correctly within a reasonable amount of time, you may be stopped at this point.

If you stop or struggle with any words, the interviewer may ask that you read another sentence or two. You must read at least one of them correctly. You needn't rush. In fact trying to read out loud too quickly can actually cause many people to make mistakes even when they can read English quite well. Pretend you are reading to your family or friends.

If you are nervous about speaking or reading English at your interview, practice at home beforehand. You can even work on your English skills by yourself by using a digital recorder. It doesn't matter if you speak with an accent as long as you speak clearly and correctly.

Some people find the written tests to be the most difficult part of the naturalization process. The good news is that the test to judge your ability to write in English is very short. The interviewer will **dictate** a sentence that you must write. Once again, the words you will be asked to write should be familiar. Like the words used in your reading test, many of these words may relate to history and government.

Grammar, punctuation, and spelling are important, but a small mistake shouldn't keep you from passing. The most important thing is that you can express the meaning of the sentence. If you don't write the first sentence correctly, you will be given two more chances. If you practice, though, you may not even need to write more than the first.

You can prepare for the English portions of your citizenship test in several ways. One very smart step is to take ESL classes. Short for English as a Second Language, these classes can be found in numerous schools and community centers around the United States. Many adult education programs and community colleges even offer special courses on preparing for the citizenship exam. Libraries can be wonderful resources for both study materials and class schedule information. Most ESL classes are offered for a small fee. Some are even free.

Another smart way to prepare for your English tests is to speak English as often as you can. Strike up a short

Many immigrants take classes to prepare for their naturalization tests. Martha Johnson is from Liberia. She is seen on the right above, attending an American history and civics class in Chelsea, Massachusetts.

conversation with a cashier, a waiter or waitress, or the person standing behind you when you have to wait in a long line. Even when you are at home with your family, make a point of using English instead of your native language as much as possible. This practice will help you understand and speak English more easily.

Your interviewer will test you on US government and history by asking you up to ten questions. The best part about this exam is that you will be given all the questions and answers beforehand. There are one hundred possible questions that the interviewer may ask you. You can download a list of all of them at the USCIS website. You will also find other helpful study materials there, including flash cards and videos.

What you won't know before your interview is which questions your interviewer will choose from the list. You must get at least six of these questions correct in order to pass this portion of the citizenship interview. This makes studying especially important. Classes that focus on preparing for the citizenship test may offer practice tests that are useful for identifying which questions you may need to study more. If you fail any part of the citizenship exam, you can take just

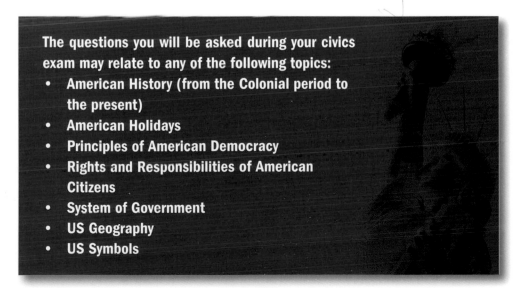

The questions you will be asked during your civics exam may relate to any of the following topics:
- **American History (from the Colonial period to the present)**
- **American Holidays**
- **Principles of American Democracy**
- **Rights and Responsibilities of American Citizens**
- **System of Government**
- **US Geography**
- **US Symbols**

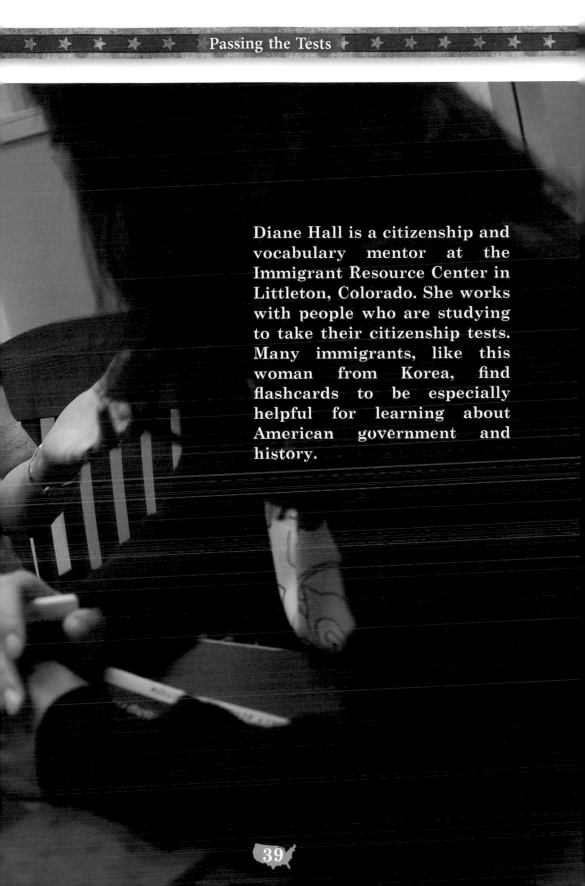

Diane Hall is a citizenship and vocabulary mentor at the Immigrant Resource Center in Littleton, Colorado. She works with people who are studying to take their citizenship tests. Many immigrants, like this woman from Korea, find flashcards to be especially helpful for learning about American government and history.

Originally from Taiwan, Sharon Hu lives in Soldotna, Alaska. On July 2, 2010, she was naturalized in a ceremony in Anchorage. Sharon and forty-nine other immigrants from twenty-seven countries became citizens on that day. Here, Sharon takes the Oath of Allegiance while holding her two-year-old son Walter.

that portion of the test again within ninety days without having to reapply.[1]

After your interview, you'll receive your results the same day. If your application is approved, you will need to attend an oath ceremony. You may be able to attend this ceremony the same day as your interview in certain areas. If not, you will receive written notice of the date, time, and location for this important event. Although the actual ceremony only takes about fifteen minutes, you should plan to spend two or three hours from the time you arrive until the time you receive your Certificate of Naturalization. Often large numbers of people take their oaths together, and it can be a lengthy process to check everyone in prior to the start of the ceremony. At the end of the ceremony, you will be asked to raise your right hand and repeat the Oath of Allegiance. Once you have repeated these important words, you will officially be a United States citizen.

Some religions prevent a person from swearing the full Oath of Allegiance during the citizenship ceremony. Jehovah's Witnesses and Quakers, for example, are both forbidden to swear oaths. In these cases, new citizens can replace the words "on oath" with "solemnly affirm."[2]

Don't be surprised if you become emotional on this special day. Many people do. In July 2012, seven hundred people from ninety-eight different countries attended a large swearing-in ceremony in Alexandria, Virginia. Jay Sandrugu, one of the new US citizens at the event, was simply overjoyed. "I am so happy. I'm so delighted. This is the best day in my life," he exclaimed.[3]

Chapter 1: The Decision to Become a US Citizen

1. Ana Gonzalez-Barrera et al., Pew Research Hispanic Center, "The Path Not Taken," February 4, 2013, http://www.pewhispanic. org/2013/02/04/the-path-not-taken/

2. Jon Roland, Constitution Society, "Presidential Eligibility," November 28, 2012, http://constitution.org/abus/pres_elig.htm

3. US Citizenship and Immigration Services, "Naturalization Oath of Allegiance to the United States of America," September 4, 2012, http://www.uscis.gov/portal/site/uscis/menuitem.5af9 bb95919f35e66f614176543f6d1a/?vgnextoid=facd6 db8d7e37210VgnVCM100000082ca60aRCRD&vgnext channel=dd7ffe9dd4aa3210VgnVCM100000b92ca60aRCRD

4. Shawna Thomas, NBC News, "Obama Urges Immigration Reform at Citizenship Ceremony," July 4, 2012, http://firstread.nbcnews. com/_news/2012/07/04/12564338-obama-urges-immigration-reform-at-citizenship-ceremony?lite

Chapter 2: Are You Eligible for Citizenship?

1. Atossa Araxia Abrahamian, *The New York Times*, "Green Card Lottery," August 17, 2012, http://www.nytimes.com/2012/08/19/ opinion/sunday/home-is-where-the-green-card-is.html? pagewanted=all&_r=0

2. Ibid.

Chapter 3: The Application Process

1. Julia Preston, *The New York Times*, "Fee Increase for Immigration Papers Planned," June 9, 2010, http://www.nytimes. com/2010/06/10/us/politics/10immig.html?ref=citizenshipand immigrationservicesus&_r=0

Chapter 4: Waiting—and Waiting Some More

1. Brent Walth and Kim Christensen, *The Oregonian*, "INS Bureaucracy, Blundering Create 'The Agency from Hell,' " December 11, 2000.

Chapter 5: Passing the Tests

1. US Citizenship and Immigration Services, "Study for the Test," http://www.uscis.gov/portal/site/uscis/menuitem.749cabd81f5 ffc8fba713d10526e0aa0/?vgnextoid=5efcebb7d4ff8210 VgnVCM10000025e6a00aRCRD&vgnextchannel=5efcebb7d4ff8210 VgnVCM10000025e6a00aRCRD

2. US Citizenship and Immigration Services, USCIS Policy Manual, "Chapter 3: Oath of Allegiance Modifications and Waivers," http://www.uscis.gov/policymanual/HTML/Policy Manual-Volume12-PartJ-Chapter3.html

3. Ben Eisler, WLJA, "Naturalization Ceremony Held in Alexandria," July 17, 2012, http://wj.la/M7OUAE

Books

Bliss, Bill. *Voices of Freedom: English and Civics for U.S. Citizenship*. White Plains, NY: Pearson Education ESL, 2010.

Sobel, Syl. *How the U.S. Government Works . . . and How It All Comes Together to Make a Nation*. Hauppauge, NY: Barron's Educational Series, 2012.

On the Internet

The United States Department of Justice, Executive Office for Immigration Review: "Free Legal Services Providers"

http://www.justice.gov/eoir/probono/states.htm

USCIS: "The Citizenship Interview and Test." YouTube video, November 2, 2010.

http://youtu.be/SDb9_CqPUTQ

US Citizenship and Immigration Services

http://www.uscis.gov/

US Citizenship and Immigration Services: "Find Help in Your Community"

http://www.uscis.gov/portal/site/uscis/menuitem.749cabd81f5ffc
8fba713d10526e0aa0/?vgnextoid=b8bade58171ed210VgnVCM
100000082ca60aRCRD&vgnextchannel=10dc9a485510e210Vgn
VCM100000082ca60aRCRD

US Citizenship and Immigration Services: "Study for the Test"

http://www.uscis.gov/portal/site/uscis/menuitem.749cabd81f5ffc
8fba713d10526e0aa0/?vgnextoid=5efcebb7d4ff8210VgnVCM
10000025e6a00aRCRD&vgnextchannel=5efcebb7d4ff8210Vgn
VCM10000025e6a00aRCRD

US Department of Health & Human Services: "Poverty Guidelines, Research, and Measurement"

http://aspe.hhs.gov/poverty/index.cfm

Works Consulted

Abrahamian, Atossa Araxia. "Green Card Lottery." *The New York Times*, August 17, 2012. http://www.nytimes.com/2012/08/19/opinion/sunday/home-is-where-the-green-card-is.html?pagewanted=all&_r=0

Bray, Ilona. *Becoming A U.S. Citizen: A Guide to the Law, Exam, and Interview.* Berkeley, CA: Nolo Publications, 2010.

Eisler, Ben. "Naturalization Ceremony Held in Alexandria." WLJA, July 17, 2012. http://wj.la/M7OUAE

Gonzalez-Barrera, Ana, Mark Hugo Lopez, Jeffrey Passel, and Paul Taylor. "The Path Not Taken." Pew Research Hispanic Center, February 4, 2013. http://www.pewhispanic.org/2013/02/04/the-path-not taken/

Roland, Jon. "Presidential Eligibility." Constitution Society, November 28, 2012. http://constitution.org/abus/pres_elig.htm.

Sicard, Cheri. *U.S. Citizenship for Dummies.* New York: Wiley Publishing, 2003.

Thomas, Shawna. "Obama Urges Immigration Reform at Citizenship Ceremony." NBC News, July 4, 2012. http://firstread.nbcnews.com/_news/2012/07/04/12564338-obama-urges-immigration-reform-at-citizenship-ceremony?lite

US Citizenship and Immigration Services. "After a Green Card is Granted." May 13, 2011. http://www.uscis.gov/portal/site/uscis/menuitem.eb1d4c2a3e5b9ac89243c6a7543f6d1a/?vgnextoid=f1903a4107083210VgnVCM100000082ca60aRCRD&vgnextchannel=f1903a4107083210VgnVCM100000082ca60aRCRD

US Citizenship and Immigration Services. "Chapter 3: Oath of Allegiance Modifications and Waivers." USCIS Policy Manual. http://www.uscis.gov/policymanual/HTML/PolicyManual-Volume12-PartJ-Chapter3.html

US Citizenship and Immigration Services. "Naturalization Oath of Allegiance to the United States of America." September 4, 2012. http://www.uscis.gov/portal/site/uscis/menuitem.5af9bb95919f35e66f614176543f6d1a/?vgnextoid=facd6db8d7e37210VgnVCM100000082ca60aRCRD&vgnextchannel=dd7ffe9dd4aa3210VgnVCM100000b92ca60aRCRD

US Citizenship and Immigration Services. "Study for the Test." http://www.uscis.gov/portal/site/uscis/menuitem.749cabd81f5ffc8fba713d10526e0aa0/?vgnextoid=5cfcebb7d4ff8210VgnVCM10000025e6a00aRCRD&vgnextchannel=5efcebb7d4ff8210VgnVCM10000025e6a00aRCRD

appeal (uh-PEEL)—A request for a legal decision to be reviewed by a higher authority.

biometrics (bahy-uh-ME-triks)—The process of detecting a person's unique physical characteristics, such as fingerprints.

dictate (DIK-teyt)—To say or read something aloud so another person can write it down.

eligible (EL-i-juh-buhl)—Meeting the requirements.

fluent (FLOO-uhnt)—Able to speak or write easily.

immigrant (IM-i-gruhnt)—A person who enters one country from another with the purpose of settling there.

minute (mahy-NOOT)—Extremely small.

naturalization (nach-er-uh-lahyz-AY-shuhn)—The process of making a person a citizen of a country.

poverty level (POV-er-tee LEV-uhl)—The official level of income that determines poorness.

waiver (WEY-ver)—An exception to a rule or law.

About the
AUTHOR

Tammy Gagne is the author of numerous books for adults and children, including *A Kid's Guide to the Voting Process* and *Life on the Reservations* for Mitchell Lane Publishers. She resides in northern New England with her husband and son. One of her favorite pastimes is visiting schools to speak to kids about the writing process.